CU00459559

PLANT BASED DIET COOKBOOK

FOR BEGINNERS

Soup, Stew and Salad Recipes.

Cook Up the Perfect Combination of Goodness, Flavors and Comfort

By Lisa Oliveri

Table of Contents

Plant Base Diet Guide Line 7

Soups and Stews 15

1   Lentil Soup 17

2   Beet Soup..18

3   Veggie Stew 19

4   Carrot Soup with Tempeh 21

5   Creamy Artichoke Soup 23

6   Tomato Artichoke Soup 25

7   Beans and Pasta Stew........................ 26

8   Barley and Lentils Soup 28

9   Cream of Miso and Mushroom Stew 30

10   Root Vegetable Stew 32

11   Curry Lentil Soup........................ 34

12   Balsamic Lentil Stew........................ 36

13   Anasazi Bean and Vegetable Stew 38

14   Lentil and Wild Rice Soup 40

15   Garlic and White Bean Soup........................ 42

16   Broccoli Cheese Soup........................ 44

17   Leek and Potato Soup 46

18   Wild Mushroom Soup........................ 48

19   Tuscan Bean Soup........................ 50

20   Traditional Mnazaleh Stew.......................... 52

Salads..55

21   Chickpea Pecan Salad 57

22   Kale Salad.. 58

23   Zucchini and Carrot Salad 59

24   Lentil Tabouli Salad................................61

25   Tomato and Cucumber Salad 63

26   Autumn Salad 64

27   Pearl Couscous Salad................................. 65

28   High Protein Salad....................................67

29   Marinated Veggie Salad.............................. 69

30   Mediterranean Salad 71

31   Pea Salad...72

32   Snap Pea Salad..74

33   Zucchini and Lentil Salad 75

34   Greek Salad 77

35   Cashew Salad with Peanut Sauce 79

36   Root Vegetable Salad 82

37   Pasta and Veggie Salad 84

38   Chickpea and Veggie Salad........................ 86

39   Farro and Veggie Salad.............................. 88

40   Bean and Couscous Salad 89

41   Roasted Beet and Avocado Salad 91

42   Cucumber and Pear Rice Salad 93

43   Tempeh and Tofu Salad............................... 94

44   Quinoa and Broccoli Salad 96

45   Greek Potato Salad 98

46   Black Bean Taco Salad Bowl...................... 100

47   Lentil Salad with Red Wine Vinaigrette.....103

48   Caviar Salad 106

49   Creamed Green Bean Salad with Pine Nuts 108

50   Old Fashion Green Bean Salad................... 110

When people see the word plant-based, they often feel as though they are going to live off salad for the rest of their lives. Yes, salad is always an excellent choice and can be very delicious when made the proper way; but this is not going to be your only food source; you are not a rabbit!

A plant-based diet is based around eating whole plant foods. This means you will be cutting out all of the highly refined foods like oil, refined sugar, and bleached flour. On top of cutting these foods out, you will also begin to minimize or exclude how much egg, dairy products, and meat you eat! Instead, you will be able to enjoy whole grains, vegetables, fruits and all types of legumes.

The key to a successful plant-based diet is to gift yourself with a variety in your diet. Leafy-vegetables are going to be important, but those alone simply do not add up to enough calories! When you think about it, you would have to consume pounds upon pounds of kale to even reach your calorie goals. Calories are important because, with not enough of them, you will end up feeling deprived and exhausted. For that reason, the plant-based diet is filled with delicious foods for you to try for yourself!

Benefits of a Plant-Based Diet

When people begin a diet, it is typically because they want to change something, and their current diet just isn't doing the trick. If this sounds like you, you are not alone! Whether your goal includes losing weight, improving your energy levels, or helping out a health issue you have, a plant-based diet may be able to benefit you.

Weight Loss

One of the major reasons men and women alike begin a plant-based diet is for the weight loss benefits! Unfortunately, around 69% of adults in the United States fall under the overweight and obese category. Fortunately, all of that can change by making the proper lifestyle and diet changes!

As you begin to adopt a plant-based diet, you will begin to eat foods that are naturally lower in calories and higher in fiber. This means that you will be eating less, getting full quicker, and staying full for a longer period of time. The fewer calories you take in, the more weight you are going to lose!

Diabetes

As you begin to eat whole foods, this will automatically provide you with the proper vitamins and minerals to boost your health. There was a study completed on 200,000 individuals where it was found that individuals who followed a plant-based diet have a 34% lowered risk of developing type 2 diabetes compared to individuals who followed a standard American diet. This could be due to the fact that a plant-based diet has the ability to improve blood sugar control.

Cognitive Power

Some whole foods you will be enjoying on a plant-based diet will have a higher number of antioxidants. Studies have found that these plant compounds and antioxidants may be the key to slowing down the progression of Alzheimer's disease and other cognitive issues. In fact, there was another study performed on 31,000 individuals who follow a plant-based lifestyle, and they had a reduced risk of 20% for developing cognitive impairment in the first place!

Heart Disease

One of the top qualities a plant-based diet is known for is being very heart-healthy. These studies about the plant-based diet rotate directly around the types of food that is being consumed, along with the quality of the food. It was found that whole foods such as legumes, nuts, whole-grains, vegetables, and fruits are all key to lowering one's risk of developing heart disease. This study was compared to those who ate refined foods like refined grains, fruit juices, and sugary drinks, which are all associated with increasing the risk of heart disease. When you eat the right foods, you get the best results!

Of course, there are many other incredible benefits that a plant-based diet can offer you, but the four above are some of the more popular reasons that people begin the diet in the first place!

Guide to Meal Planning

While meal planning can seem complicated, the key to success is making it as simple as possible! Especially if you are just starting out, there is no need to overwhelm yourself! The only way you are going to experience the benefits of a plant-based diet is if you stick to your diet! As you begin, I don't want you to feel like you are torturing yourself! A new diet is meant to give you a new lease on life. You will be eating better foods, trying new things, and getting healthier along the way! For this reason, try not to put too much stress on yourself!

Believe it or not, you are going to goof up a lot! Welcome to being human! We are creatures of habit, so we like to eat the same foods we have been eating our whole life. Luckily, through hard work and dedication, you can change these habits and help yourself become healthier! Let's face it, when it comes down to it, you are most likely the only one putting food in your mouth! Your results are completely in your hands.

Step One:

Write it down! With the internet, there are plenty of online resources. You will want to take a few moments to find a planning sheet. Often times, when we keep something or plan something in our head, it is easy to get buried with the million other responsibilities you have that day. Instead, take the time to write your meal plan down; that way, it is right in front of you when you need it!

Step Two:

We all have busy schedules, but this doesn't mean that you shouldn't take some of that precious time for yourself! When you are making your plan, you will want to look for events the week before. Is there a work meeting or party that could get in the way of a meal? That is perfectly okay; all you have to do is plan for it!

When people first begin a plant-based diet, they are fearful of going out and being social. The good news is that in the modern age, a number of different restaurants are becoming more plant-based friendly. If you do have a social event, try to make a plan! You can go on their website to check out their menu ahead of time or simply ask a few questions before you order. As long as the meal is as little processed as possible, you will stay on the right track!

Step Three:

If you are just starting out, I suggest only planning for one meal. Whether that be breakfast, lunch, or dinner, choose something that will typically take you the most time. When you plan ahead, this will help save you time in the long run! For this reason, I typically choose dinner. For breakfast and lunch, you can keep it extremely simple. Lunch is especially easy to plan for because you can either have a salad or the dinner leftovers!

Step Four:

Once you have your meal picked out, plan it out for the week! As a beginner, you may only want to plan for one or two days the first week. As you become more comfortable with your diet, you can plan for more! All you will have to do is select two recipes from this book, choose the two days you want to make these meals, and you are on your way to becoming a meal planning expert!

Step Five:

Once you have your recipes selected and your meal plan set, take the time to write up a shopping list before you even hit the store. This will assure you stick to your list instead of grabbing random ingredients that will just go bad at the end of the week because you didn't use it! Meal planning has the ability to save you time and money when you work on doing it properly!

Shopping List

If you are looking for a place to start, below you will find a shopping list that contains some good staples to keep in your fridge and cabinets. Keep in mind that most of these foods are going to be perishable. While this may seem like a pitfall, fresh produce is going to be much healthier for you compared to the foods that have additives to keep their shelf life. With that in mind, meal planning is going to be important to keep you from wasting food and money!

Fruit:

Melon, Bananas, Apples, Lemons, Limes, Oranges, Grapes, Mixed Berries

Vegetables:

Asparagus, Avocado, Tomatoes, Onions, Sweet Potatoes, Regular Potatoes, Cauliflower, Broccoli, Mushrooms, Lettuce, Kale, Carrots, Squash

Cooking Items:

Nutritional Yeast, Plant-based Milk, Seasonings, Maple Syrup, Stevia

Pantry Items:

Black Beans, Chickpeas, Whole Grain Pasta, Risotto, Whole Grain Pasta, Oats, Kidney Beans, Nuts, Seeds

With all of this in mind, it is now time to get to the best part of the plant-based diet; the recipes! Whether you are looking for a meal, snack, or dessert, this book has got you covered! As you flip through the recipes, jot down some of your favorites! The hardest part is getting started, but once you begin, there will be no stopping you or the incredible results that come with the diet. When you are ready, let's take a look.

Preparation Time: 10 Minutes
Cooking Time: 40-45 Minutes
Servings: 2
Ingredients:
Dressing:

- ¾ cup of vegetable broth
- 1 carrot, sliced
- 1 onion, diced
- 2 bay leaves
- ¼ tsp of dried thyme
- 1 tsp of olive oil
- 1/3 pound of brown lentils
- 2 tsp of lemon juice
- Salt & pepper, to taste

Directions:

1. Sauté carrot and onion in sunflower oil on a medium heat for around 5 minutes or until onions have become translucent.
2. Add lentils, bay leaves, thyme, salt & pepper, and vegetable broth. Lower heat and simmer. Put the lid on and allow to cook for about 40 to 45 minutes, just to make sure the lentils have softened.
3. Take the leaves out, and stir the lemon juice in.
4. Serve hot.

Nutrition: Calories: 398; Fats: 2g; Carbohydrates: 70; Protein: 25g

2 Beet Soup

Preparation Time: 10 Minutes

Cooking Time: 5 Minutes

Servings: 2

Ingredients:

- 2 cups coconut yogurt
- 4 teaspoons fresh lemon juice
- 2 cups beets, trimmed, peeled, and chopped
- 2 tablespoons fresh dill
- Salt, to taste
- 1 tablespoon pumpkin seeds
- 2 tablespoons coconut cream
- 1 tablespoon fresh chives, minced

Directions:

1. In a high-speed blender, add all ingredients and pulse until smooth.
2. Transfer the soup into a pan over medium heat and cook for about 3–5 minutes or until heated through.
3. Serve immediately with the garnishing of chives and coconut cream.

Nutrition: Calories: 230; Fat: 8g; Carbohydrates: 33.5g; Protein: 8g

Preparation Time: 15 Minutes

Cooking Time: 30 Minutes

Servings: 3

Ingredients:

- 2 tablespoons olive oil
- 1 large onion, chopped
- 2 garlic cloves, minced
- ¼ teaspoon fresh ginger, grated finely
- 1 teaspoon ground cumin
- 1 teaspoon cayenne pepper
- Salt and ground black pepper, to taste
- 2 cups homemade vegetable broth
- 1½ cups small broccoli florets
- 1½ cups small cauliflower florets
- 1 tablespoon fresh lemon juice
- 1 cup cashews
- 1 teaspoon fresh lemon zest, grated finely

Directions:

1. In a large soup pan, heat oil over medium heat and sauté the onion for about 3–4 minutes.
2. Add the garlic, ginger, and spices and sauté for about 1 minute.

3. Add 1 cup of the broth and bring to a boil.
4. Add the vegetables and again bring to a boil.
5. Cover the soup pan and cook for about 15–20 minutes, stirring occasionally.
6. Stir in the lemon juice and remove from the heat.
7. Serve hot with the topping of cashews and lemon zest.

Nutrition: Calories: 425; Protein: 13g; Carbohydrates: 27g; Fat: 32g

Preparation Time: 15 Minutes

Cooking Time: 45 Minutes

Servings: 6

Ingredients:

- ¼ cup olive oil, divided
- 1 large yellow onion, chopped
- Salt, to taste
- 2 pounds carrots, peeled, and cut into ½-inch rounds
- 2 tablespoons fresh dill, chopped
- 4½ cups homemade vegetable broth
- 12 ounces tempeh, cut into ½-inch cubes
- ¼ cup tomato paste
- 1 teaspoon fresh lemon juice

Directions:

1. In a large soup pan, heat 2 tablespoons of the oil over medium heat and cook the onion with salt for about 6–8 minutes, stirring frequently.
2. Add the carrots and stir to combine.
3. Lower the heat to low and cook, covered for about 5 minutes, stirring frequently.
4. Add in the broth and bring to a boil over high heat.

5. Lower the heat to a low and simmer, covered for about 30 minutes.

6. Meanwhile, in a skillet, heat the remaining oil over medium-high heat and cook the tempeh for about 3–5 minutes.

7. Stir in the dill and cook for about 1 minute.

8. Remove from the heat.

9. Remove the pan of soup from heat and stir in tomato paste and lemon juice.

10. With an immersion blender, blend the soup until smooth and creamy.

11. Serve the soup hot with the topping of tempeh.

Nutrition: Calories: 294; Fat: 15.7g; Carbohydrates: 26; Protein: 16g

Preparation Time: 5 Minutes

Cooking Time: 40 Minutes

Servings: 4

Ingredients:

- 1 can artichoke hearts, drained
- 3 cups vegetable broth
- 2 tbsp. lemon juice
- 1 small onion, finely cut
- 2 cloves garlic, crushed
- 3 tbsp. olive oil
- 2 tbsp. flour
- ½ cup vegan cream

Directions:

1. Gently sauté the onion and garlic in some olive oil. Add the flour, whisking constantly, and then add the hot vegetable broth slowly, while still whisking. Cook for about 5 minutes.

2. Blend the artichoke, lemon juice, salt, and pepper until smooth. Add the puree to the broth mix, stir well, and then stir in the cream. Cook until heated through. Garnish with a swirl of vegan cream or a sliver of artichoke.

Nutrition: Calories: 162; Fat: 18g; Carbohydrates: 11; Protein: 4g

Preparation Time: 5 Minutes

Cooking Time: 35 minutes

Servings: 4

Ingredients:

- 1 can artichoke hearts, drained
- 1 can diced tomatoes, undrained
- 3 cups vegetable broth
- 1 small onion, chopped
- 2 cloves garlic, crushed
- 1 tbsp. pesto
- Black pepper, to taste

Directions:

1. Combine all ingredients in the slow cooker.
2. Cover and cook on low for 8-10 hours or on high for 4-5 hours.
3. Blend the soup in batches then put it back to the slow cooker. Season with pepper and salt, then serve.

Nutrition: Calories: 148; Fat: 16g; Carbohydrates: 8.2; Protein: 4g

Preparation Time: 15 Minutes

Cooking Time: 35 minutes

Servings: 6

Ingredients:

- ¼ cup canola oil
- 1 large yellow onion, chopped
- 1 potato, chopped
- 8 ounces fresh shiitake mushrooms, sliced
- 1 medium tomato, chopped
- 2 tablespoons garlic, chopped finely
- 2 bay leaves
- 2 tablespoons mixed Italian herbs (rosemary, thyme, basil), chopped
- 1 teaspoon cayenne pepper
- 4 cups homemade vegetable broth
- 2 tablespoons apple cider vinegar
- 1 cup whole-wheat fusilli pasta
- 1/3 cup nutritional yeast
- 1/3 cup roasted tomato salsa
- 8 ounces fresh collard greens
- 1 (15-ounce) can cannellini beans, drained and rinsed

- Salt and ground black pepper, to taste

Directions:

1. In a large pan, heat the oil over medium heat and sauté the onion, mushrooms, potato, and tomato for about 4–5 minutes.
2. Add the garlic, bay leaves, herbs, and cayenne pepper and sauté for about 1 minute.
3. Add the broth and bring to a boil.
4. Stir in the vinegar, pasta, nutritional yeast, and tomato salsa and again bring to a boil.
5. Lower the heat to medium-low and simmer, covered for about 20 minutes.
6. Uncover and stir in the greens and beans.
7. Simmer for about 4–5 minutes.
8. Stir in the salt and black pepper and remove from the heat.
9. Serve hot.

Nutrition: Calories:299; Fat: 11g; Protein: 16g; Carbohydrates: 37g

Preparation Time: 20 Minutes

Cooking Time: 50 minutes

Servings: 8

Ingredients:

- 2 tablespoons olive oil
- 2 carrots, peeled and chopped
- 1 large red onion, chopped
- 2 celery stalks, chopped
- 2 garlic cloves, minced
- 1 teaspoon ground coriander
- 2 teaspoons ground cumin
- 1 teaspoon cayenne pepper
- 1 cup barley
- 1 cup red lentils
- 5 cups tomatoes, chopped finely
- 5–6 cups homemade vegetable broth
- 6 cups fresh spinach, torn
- Salt and ground black pepper, to taste

Directions:

1. In a large pan, heat the oil over medium heat and sauté the carrots, onion, and celery for about 5 minutes.

2. Add the garlic and spices and sauté for about 1 minute.
3. Add the barley, lentils, tomatoes, and broth and bring to a rolling boil.
4. Reduce the heat to low and simmer, covered for about 40 minutes.
5. Stir in the spinach, salt, and black pepper, and simmer for about 3–4 minutes.
6. Serve hot.

Nutrition: Calories: 264; Fat: 6g; Carbohydrates: 41g; Protein: 14g

Preparation Time: 5 Minutes

Cooking Time: 15 Minutes

Servings: 4-6

Ingredients:

1 tablespoon low-sodium soy sauce or tamari

1 cup julienned green onions

2 cups sliced mushrooms (shiitake, oyster, or baby bella)

2 cups miso cream sauce

2 cups vegetable broth

1 tablespoon rice vinegar

Miso Cream Sauce

½ cup raw cashews

3 tablespoons white or yellow miso paste

2 cups unsweetened soy milk, divided

¾ cup vegetable broth

Directions:

1. In a large saucepan, heat the soy sauce over medium-high heat. Add the green onions and mushrooms and sauté until tender, 3 to 5 minutes. Add the miso cream sauce and sauté until it begins to thicken, about 3 minutes.

2. Add the broth and bring to a boil. Lower the heat to low and simmer, stirring occasionally, for 10 minutes.
3. Remove from the heat. Stir in the vinegar and serve.

For a Cream of Miso:

1. In a high-speed blender, grind the cashews into a flour (be careful not to grind them into nut butter).
2. Transfer the cashew flour to a small bowl, add the miso and 1 cup of soy milk, and whisk to combine.
3. In a saucepan, bring the remaining 1 cup of soy milk and the broth to a boil over medium-high heat. Lower the heat to medium-low, add the cashew mixture, and bring to a simmer. Cook, whisking occasionally, until thick, 5 to 10 minutes.
4. Use immediately, or let cool and store in an airtight container in the refrigerator for up to 5 days.

Nutrition: Calories: 156; Fat: 7g; Carbohydrates: 13g; Protein: 8g

Preparation Time: 10 Minutes

Cooking Time: 8 Hours 10 Minutes

Servings: 6

Ingredients:

- 2 cups chopped kale
- 1 large white onion, peeled, chopped
- 1 pound parsnips, peeled, chopped
- 1 pound potatoes, peeled, chopped
- 2 celery ribs, chopped
- 1 pound butternut squash, peeled, deseeded, chopped
- 1 pound carrots, peeled, chopped
- 3 teaspoons minced garlic
- 1 pound sweet potatoes, peeled, chopped
- 1 bay leaf
- 1 teaspoon ground black pepper
- 1/2 teaspoon sea salt
- 1 tablespoon chopped sage
- 3 cups vegetable broth

Directions:

1. Switch on the slow cooker, add all the ingredients in it, except for the kale, and stir until mixed.

2. Shut the cooker with lid and cook for 8 hours at a low heat setting until cooked.
3. When done, add kale into the stew, stir until mixed, and cook for 10 minutes until leaves have wilted.
4. Serve straight away.

Nutrition: Calories: 120; Protein: 4g; Carbohydrates: 28g; Fats: 1g

11 Curry Lentil Soup

Preparation Time: 10 Minutes

Cooking Time: 40 Minutes

Servings: 6

Ingredients:

- 1 cup brown lentils
- 1 medium white onion, peeled, chopped
- 28 ounces diced tomatoes
- 1 ½ teaspoon minced garlic
- 1 inch of ginger, grated
- 3 cups vegetable broth
- 1/2 teaspoon salt
- 2 tablespoons curry powder
- 1 teaspoon cumin
- 1/2 teaspoon cayenne
- 1 tablespoon olive oil
- 1 1/2 cups coconut milk, unsweetened
- ¼ cup chopped cilantro

Directions:

1. Take a soup pot, place it over medium-high heat, add oil and when hot, add onion, stir in garlic and ginger and cook for 5 minutes until golden brown.

2. Then add all the ingredients except for milk and cilantro, stir until mixed and simmer until lentils have cooked.
3. When done, stir in milk, cook for 5 minutes until thoroughly heated and then garnish the soup with cilantro.
4. Serve straight away

Nutrition: Calories: 269; Fats: 15g; Carbohydrates: 26g; Protein: 10g

Preparation Time: 10 Minutes

Cooking Time: 30 Minutes

Servings: 5

Ingredients:

- 1 teaspoon extra-virgin olive oil
- 4 carrots, peeled and chopped
- 1 onion, chopped
- 3 garlic cloves, minced
- 2 tablespoons balsamic vinegar
- 4 cups Vegetable Broth or water
- 1 (28-ounce) can crushed tomatoes
- 1 tablespoon sugar
- 2 cups dried lentils or 2 (15-ounce) cans lentils, drained and rinsed
- 1 teaspoon salt
- Freshly ground black pepper

Directions:

1. Preparing the Ingredients
2. Heat the olive oil in a large soup pot over medium heat.
3. Add the carrots, onion, and garlic, then sauté for about 5 minutes until the vegetables are softened. Pour in the vinegar, and let it sizzle to deglaze the

bottom of the pot. Add the vegetable broth, tomatoes, sugar, and lentils.

4. Bring to a boil, then reduce the heat to low. Simmer for about 25 minutes until the lentils are soft.

5. Finish and Serve

6. Add the salt and season with pepper. Leftovers will keep in an airtight container for up to 1 week in the refrigerator, or up to 1 month in the freezer.

Nutrition: Calories: 253; Fat: 2g; Carbohydrates: 67g; Protein: 22g

13 Anasazi Bean and Vegetable Stew

Preparation Time: 15 Minutes

Cooking Time: 60 Minutes

Servings: 3

Ingredients:

- 1 cup Anasazi beans, soaked overnight and drained
- 3 cups roasted vegetable broth
- 1 bay laurel
- 1 thyme sprig, chopped
- 1 rosemary sprig, chopped
- 3 tablespoons olive oil
- 1 large onion, chopped
- 2 celery stalks, chopped
- 2 carrots, chopped
- 2 bell peppers, seeded and chopped
- 1 green chili pepper, seeded and chopped
- 2 garlic cloves, minced
- Sea salt and ground black pepper, to taste
- 1 teaspoon cayenne pepper
- 1 teaspoon paprika

Directions:

1. In a saucepan, bring the Anasazi beans and broth to a boil. Once boiling, turn the heat to a simmer. Add

in the bay laurel, thyme and rosemary; let it cook for about 50 minutes or until tender.

2. Meanwhile, in a heavy-bottomed pot, heat the olive oil over medium-high heat. Now, sauté the onion, celery, carrots and peppers for about 4 minutes until tender.

3. Add in the garlic and continue to sauté for a few seconds more or until aromatic.

4. Add the sautéed mixture to the cooked beans. Season with salt, black pepper, cayenne pepper and paprika.

5. Continue to simmer, stirring periodically, for 10 minutes more or until everything is cooked through. Bon appétit!

Nutrition: Calories: 444; Protein: 20g; Carbohydrates: 58g; Fat: 16g

Preparation Time: 5 Minutes

Cooking Time: 40 Minutes

Servings: 4

Ingredients:

- 1/2 cup cooked mixed beans
- 12 ounces cooked lentils
- 2 stalks of celery, sliced
- 1 1/2 cup mixed wild rice, cooked
- 1 large sweet potato, peeled, chopped
- 1/2 medium butternut, peeled, chopped
- 4 medium carrots, peeled, sliced
- 1 medium onion, peeled, diced
- 10 cherry tomatoes
- 1/2 red chili, deseeded, diced
- 1 ½ teaspoon minced garlic
- 1/2 teaspoon salt
- 2 teaspoons mixed dried herbs
- 1 teaspoon coconut oil
- 2 cups vegetable broth

Directions:

1. Take a large pot, place it over medium-high heat, add oil and when it melts, add onion and cook for 5 minutes.

2. Stir in garlic and chili, cook for 3 minutes, then add remaining vegetables, pour in the broth, stir and bring the mixture to a boil.

3. Switch heat to medium-low heat, cook the soup for 20 minutes, then stir in remaining ingredients and continue cooking for 10 minutes until soup has reached to desired thickness.

4. Serve straight away.

Nutrition: Calories: 331; Fat: 2g; Carbohydrates: 54g; Protein: 13g

Preparation Time: 5 Minutes

Cooking Time: 10 Minutes

Servings: 4

Ingredients:

- 45 ounces cooked cannellini beans
- 1/4 teaspoon dried thyme
- 2 teaspoons minced garlic
- 1/8 teaspoon crushed red pepper
- 1/2 teaspoon dried rosemary
- 1/8 teaspoon ground black pepper
- 2 tablespoons olive oil
- 4 cups vegetable broth

Directions:

1. Place one-third of white beans in a food processor, then pour in 2 cups broth and pulse for 2 minutes until smooth.

2. Place a pot over medium heat, add oil and when hot, add garlic and cook for 1 minute until fragrant.

3. Add pureed beans into the pan along with remaining beans, sprinkle with spices and herbs, pour in the broth, stir until combined, and bring the mixture to boil over medium-high heat.

4. Switch heat to medium-low level, simmer the beans for 15 minutes, and then mash them with a fork.

5. Taste the soup to adjust seasoning and then serve.

Nutrition: Calories: 222; Fat: 7g; Carbohydrates:13g; Protein: 11g

Preparation Time: 5 Minutes

Cooking Time: 15 minutes

Servings: 4

Ingredients:

- 1 medium potato, peeled, diced
- 2 ribs celery, diced
- 1 medium white onion, peeled, diced
- 2 medium yellow summer squash, diced
- 1 medium carrot, peeled, diced
- 6 cups chopped broccoli florets
- 1 teaspoon minced garlic
- 1 bay leaf
- 1/3 teaspoon ground black pepper
- ¼ cup nutritional yeast
- 1 tablespoon lemon juice
- 2 tablespoons apple cider vinegar
- ½ cup cashews
- 3 cups of water

Directions:

1. Take a large pot, place it over medium-high heat, add all the vegetables in it, except for florets, add bay leaf, pour in water and bring the mixture to boil.

2. Then switch heat to medium-low and simmer for 10 minutes until vegetables are tender.

3. Meanwhile, place broccoli florets in another pot, place it over medium-low heat and cook for 4 minutes or more until broccoli has steamed.

4. When done, remove broccoli from the pot, reserve 1 cup of its liquid, and set aside until required.

5. When vegetables have cooked, remove the bay leaf, add remaining ingredients in it, reserving broccoli and its liquid, and then puree the soup by using an immersion blender until smooth.

6. Then add steamed broccoli along with its liquid, stir well and serve straight away.

Nutrition: Calories: 223; Fat: 12g; Carbohydrates: 19g; Protein: 10g

Preparation Time: 5 Minutes

Cooking Time: 15 minutes

Servings: 6

Ingredients:

- 3 leeks (white and light green parts only), chopped
- 1 white or yellow onion, chopped
- 3 or 4 garlic cloves, minced
- 1 tablespoon olive oil
- 6 medium russet potatoes, scrubbed or peeled and roughly chopped (6 to 7 cups)
- ½ (13.5-ounce) can coconut milk (about ¾ cup)
- 4 cups water or unsalted vegetable broth
- ½ teaspoon salt, plus more as needed
- 1 teaspoon garlic powder (optional)
- Freshly ground black pepper

Directions:

1. Preparing the Ingredients. On your electric pressure cooker, select Sauté. Add the leeks, onion, garlic, and olive oil. Cook for 4 to 5 minutes, until the leek and onion are softened. Add the potatoes, coconut milk, water, and salt. Cancel Sauté.

2. High pressure for 7 minutes. Close and lock the lid, and select High Pressure for 7 minutes.

3. Pressure Release. Let the pressure release naturally, about 20 minutes. Unlock and remove the lid. Let cool for a few minutes and then purée the soup—either transfer the soup (in batches, if necessary) to a countertop blender. Taste and season with the garlic powder (if using), salt, and pepper.

Nutrition: Calories: 274; Fat: 10g; Protein: 5g; Carbohydrates: 75g

Preparation Time: 10 Minutes

Cooking Time: 50 minutes

Servings: 4

Ingredients:

- 3 tablespoons sesame oil
- 1 pound mixed wild mushrooms, sliced
- 1 white onion, chopped
- 3 cloves garlic, minced and divided
- 2 sprigs thyme, chopped
- 2 sprigs rosemary, chopped
- 1/4 cup flaxseed meal
- 1/4 cup dry white wine
- 3 cups vegetable broth
- 1/2 teaspoon red chili flakes
- Garlic salt and freshly ground black pepper, to seasoned

Directions:

1. Start by preheating your oven to 395 degrees F.
2. Place the mushrooms in a single layer onto a parchment-lined baking pan. Drizzle the mushrooms with 1 tablespoon of the sesame oil.
3. Roast the mushrooms in the preheated oven for about 25 minutes, or until tender.

4. Heat the remaining 2 tablespoons of the sesame oil in a stockpot over medium heat. Then, sauté the onion for about 3 minutes or until tender and translucent.
5. Then, add in the garlic, thyme and rosemary and continue to sauté for 1 minute or so until aromatic. Sprinkle flaxseed meal over everything.
6. Add in the remaining ingredients and continue to simmer for 10 to 15 minutes longer or until everything is cooked through.
7. Stir in the roasted mushrooms and continue simmering for a further 12 minutes. Ladle into soup bowls and serve hot. Enjoy!

Nutrition: Calories: 313; Fat: 23g; Carbohydrates: 14.5g; Protein: 14.5g

Preparation Time: 10 Minutes

Cooking Time: 25 Minutes

Servings: 5

Ingredients:

- 3 tablespoons olive oil
- 1 medium leek, chopped
- 1 celery with leaves, chopped
- 1 zucchini, diced
- 1 Italian pepper, sliced
- 3 garlic cloves, crushed
- 2 bay leaves
- Kosher salt and ground black pepper, to taste
- 1 teaspoon cayenne pepper
- 1 (28-ounce) can tomatoes, crushed
- 2 cups vegetable broth
- 2 (15-ounce) cans Great Northern beans, drained
- 2 cups Lacinato kale, torn into pieces
- 1 cup crostini

Directions:

1. In a heavy-bottomed pot, heat the olive oil over medium heat. Once hot, sauté the leek, celery, zucchini and pepper for about 4 minutes.

2. Sauté the garlic and bay leaves for about 1 minute or so.

3. Add in the spices, tomatoes, broth and canned beans. Let it simmer, stirring occasionally, for about 15 minutes or until cooked through.

4. Add in the Lacinato kale and continue simmering, stirring occasionally, for 4 minutes.

5. Serve garnished with crostini. Bon appétit!

Nutrition: Calories: 388; Fat: 10g; Carbohydrates: 57g; Protein: 20g

Preparation Time: 5 Minutes

Cooking Time: 25 Minutes

Servings: 14

Ingredients:

- 4 tablespoons olive oil
- 1 onion, chopped
- 1 large-sized eggplant, peeled and diced
- 1 cup carrots, chopped
- 2 garlic cloves, minced
- 2 large-sized tomatoes, pureed
- 1 teaspoon Baharat seasoning
- 2 cups vegetable broth
- 14 ounces canned chickpeas, drained
- Kosher salt and ground black pepper, to taste
- 1 medium-sized avocado, pitted, peeled and sliced

Directions:

1. In a heavy-bottomed pot, heat the olive oil over medium heat. Once hot, sauté the onion, eggplant and carrots for about 4 minutes.

2. Sauté the garlic for about 1 minute or until aromatic.

3. Add in the tomatoes, Baharat seasoning, broth and canned chickpeas. Let it simmer, stirring

occasionally, for about 20 minutes or until cooked through.

4. Season with salt and pepper. Serve garnished with slices of the fresh avocado. Bon appétit!

Nutrition: Calories: 439; Protein: 13.5g; Carbohydrates: 45g; Fats: 24g

Preparation Time: 5 Minutes

Cooking Time: 0 Minutes

Servings: 4

Ingredients:

- 1 (15-ounce) can chickpeas, drained and rinsed
- 1 (4-ounce) jar hearts of palm, drained
- ½ teaspoon ground thyme
- ½ teaspoon ground sage
- 1 large celery stalk, chopped
- ¼ cup dried cranberries
- 2 tablespoons rice vinegar
- ¼ cup chopped pecans

Directions:

1 Place the chickpeas and hearts of palm in a food processor and pulse in 1-second bursts until the mixture has a flaky texture. Be careful not to overprocess. Transfer the mixture to a medium bowl.

2 Add the thyme, sage, celery, cranberries, vinegar, and pecans and stir to combine.

3 Serve immediately, or store in an airtight container in the refrigerator for up to 5 days.

Nutrition: Calories: 225; Fats: 1g; Carbohydrates: 35g; Protein: 8g

Preparation Time: 10 Minutes

Cooking Time: 0 Minutes

Servings: 4

Ingredients:

- 2 bunches kale, leaves stemmed and torn into bite-size pieces
- ¼ cup tahini
- ¼ cup lemon juice
- 2 garlic cloves, minced
- ¼ cup hemp seeds
- 1 teaspoon salt

Directions:

1 Place the kale in a large bowl. Add the tahini, lemon juice, and garlic. With clean or gloved hands, massage the kale until it brightens and glistens and the leaves are coated, about 3 minutes.

2 Sprinkle the hemp seeds and salt over the salad and toss gently, then serve.

Nutrition: Calories: 162; Fat: 2g; Carbohydrates: 9g; Protein: 6g

Preparation Time: 10 Minutes

Cooking Time: 0 Minutes

Servings: 6

Ingredients:

For the Salad:

- 2 scallions, sliced

- 2 large zucchini. spiralized

- 1 red chile, sliced

- 1 large carrot, spiralized

For the Dressing:

- 1 1/2 teaspoon grated ginger

- 2 teaspoons brown sugar

- 1/4 cup lime juice

- 1 tablespoon soy sauce

- 2 tablespoons toasted peanut oil

For Toppings:

- 1/2 cup chopped peanuts, roasted

- 1/3 cup chopped cilantro

Directions:

1 Prepare the dressing and for this, place all of its ingredients in a bowl and whisk until combined.

2   Take a large bowl, place all the ingredients for the salad in it, stir until mixed, then drizzle with the dressing and toss until coated.

3   Top the salad with nuts and cilantro and then serve straight away.

Nutrition: Calories: 150; Protein: 5g; Carbohydrates: 11g; Fat: 11g

Preparation Time: 10 Minutes

Cooking Time: 15 Minutes

Servings: 4

Ingredients:

For the Salad:

- 1 1/2 cups puy lentils, cooked
- 1/3 cup diced red onion
- 2 cups diced tomatoes
- 1/4 cup chopped mint
- 1 1/2 cups chopped parsley

For the Dressing:

- 1/3 teaspoon ground black pepper
- 1 teaspoon cinnamon
- 1 teaspoon salt
- 2 teaspoon allspice
- 3 tablespoons olive oil
- 1 lemon, juiced, zested

Directions:

1 Prepare the dressing and for this, place all of its ingredients in a small bowl and whisk until smooth.

2 Take a large bowl, place all the ingredients for the salad in it, top with prepared dressing and toss until well coated.

3   Let the salad stand for 10 minutes and then serve.

Nutrition: Calories: 319; Fat: 9.5g; Carbohydrates: 46g; Protein: 16g

Preparation Time: 5 Minutes

Cooking Time: 0 Minutes

Servings: 2

Ingredients:

- 4 Tomatoes, cut into wedges
- 2 Cucumber, sliced
- 1 Onion, medium, peeled, chopped
- 1/3 teaspoon Salt
- ¼ teaspoon Ground black pepper
- 1 tablespoon Parsley, chopped

Directions:

1. Take a large bowl, place all the ingredients for the salad in it and then toss until combined.
2. Serve straight away.

Nutrition: Calories: 97; Fat: 0g; Carbohydrates: 23g; Protein: 1g

26 Autumn Salad

Preparation Time: 5 Minutes

Cooking Time: 0 Minutes

Servings: 6

Ingredients:

- 2 diced ripe pears
- 8 ounces of mixed greens (arugula, baby spinach, baby greens, radicchio, etc.)
- 1 ounce of pecan halves
- 2 tablespoons of red wine vinegar
- 1 teaspoon of maple syrup
- ½ teaspoon of Dijon mustard
- 3 tablespoons of extra virgin olive oil
- ¼ teaspoon of sea salt
- Black pepper, to taste

Directions:

1. Whisk mustard, maple syrup, vinegar, olive oil, pepper, and salt in a large bowl until combined.
2. Mix greens, pecans, and pears in a salad bowl.
3. Add the prepared sauce in the salad bowl and toss well.
4. Serve and enjoy your Autumn Salad!

Nutrition: Calories: 160; Fat: 12g; Carbohydrates: 10g; Protein: 4.5g

Preparation Time: 10 Minutes

Cooking Time: 20 Minutes

Servings: 5

Ingredients:

- 3/4 cup of whole-wheat pearl couscous
- 1 ½ cups of quartered grape tomatoes
- ¾ pound of thin asparagus spears
- ¼ cup of chopped red onion
- 1 ½ juiced lemons
- 2 tablespoons of chopped parsley
- 1 tablespoon of extra virgin olive oil
- Sea salt, to taste
- Black pepper, to taste

Directions:

1. Pour water to a large pot, add salt, and bring it to a boil. Add in asparagus and cook for 3 minutes until tender.
2. Take out asparagus with a slotted spoon and rinse it under cold running water.
3. Cook couscous in the boiling water according to package directions.
4. Cut the cooked asparagus into ½-inch pieces.

5. Drain couscous and rinse it under cold running water. Put it in a large bowl.

6. Add vegetables, olive oil, lemon juice, parsley, pepper, and salt to the bowl and toss.

7. Serve and enjoy!

Nutrition: Calories: 170; Fat: 4g; Protein: 6.5g; Carbohydrates: 30g

Preparation Time: 5 Minutes

Cooking Time: 5 Minutes

Servings: 4

Ingredients:

Salad:

- 15-oz can green kidney beans
- 4 tbsp capers
- 4 handfuls arugula
- 15-oz can lentils

Dressing:

- 1 tbsp caper brine
- 1 tbsp tamari
- 1 tbsp balsamic vinegar
- 2 tbsp peanut butter
- 2 tbsp hot sauce
- 1 tbsp tahini

Directions:

1. For the dressing:
2. In a bowl, stir all together all the ingredients until they come together to form a smooth dressing.
3. For the salad:
4. Mix the beans, arugula, capers, and lentils. Top with the dressing and serve.

Nutrition: Calories: 205; Fat: 2g; Carbohydrates: 31g; Protein: 13g

Preparation Time: 4 Hours 30 Minutes

Cooking Time: 3 Minutes

Servings: 6

Ingredients:

- 1 zucchini, sliced
- 4 tomatoes, sliced into wedges
- ¼ cup red onion, sliced thinly
- 1 green bell pepper, sliced
- 2 tablespoons fresh parsley, chopped
- 2 tablespoons red-wine vinegar
- 2 tablespoons olive oil
- 1 clove garlic, minced
- 1 teaspoon dried basil
- 1 tablespoons water
- Pine nuts, toasted and chopped

Directions:

1. In a bowl, combine the zucchini, tomatoes, red onion, green bell pepper, and parsley.
2. Pour the vinegar and oil into a glass jar with a lid.
3. Add the garlic, basil, and water.
4. Seal the jar and stir well to combine.
5. Pour the dressing into the vegetable mixture.
6. Cover the bowl.

7. Marinate in the refrigerator for 4 hours.

8. Garnish with the pine nuts before serving.

Nutrition: Calories: 65; Fat: 5g; Carbohydrates: 5g; Protein: 1g

Preparation Time: 20 Minutes

Cooking Time: 5 Minutes

Servings: 2

Ingredients:

- 2 teaspoons balsamic vinegar
- 1 tablespoon basil pesto
- 1 cup lettuce
- ¼ cup broccoli florets, chopped
- ½ cup zucchini, chopped
- ¼ cup tomato, chopped
- ¼ cup yellow bell pepper, chopped
- 2 tablespoons feta cheese, crumbled

Directions:

1. Arrange the lettuce on a serving platter.
2. Top with the broccoli, zucchini, tomato, and bell pepper.
3. In a bowl, mix the vinegar and pesto.
4. Drizzle the dressing on top.
5. Sprinkle the feta cheese and serve.

Nutrition: Calories: 100; Protein: 4g; Carbohydrates: 7g; Fats: 6g

Preparation Time: 40 Minutes

Cooking Time: 0 Minutes

Servings: 6

Ingredients:

- 1 cup chickpeas, rinsed and drained
- 1 ½ cups peas, divided
- Salt to taste
- 3 tablespoons olive oil
- ½ cup buttermilk
- Pepper to taste
- 8 cups pea greens
- 3 carrots shaved
- 1 cup snow peas, trimmed

Directions:

1 Add the chickpeas and half of the peas to your food processor.

2 Season with the salt.

3 Pulse until smooth. Set aside.

4 In a bowl, toss the remaining peas in oil, milk, salt, and pepper.

5 Transfer the mixture to your food processor.

6 Process until pureed.

7 Transfer this mixture to a bowl.

8 Arrange the pea greens on a serving plate.

9 Top with the shaved carrots and snow peas.

10 Stir in the pea and milk dressing.

11 Serve with the reserved chickpea hummus.

Nutrition: Calories: 214; Fats: 9g.; Carbohydrates: 27g; Protein: 8g

32 Snap Pea Salad

Preparation Time: 60 Minutes

Cooking Time: 0 Minutes

Servings: 6

Ingredients:

- 2 tablespoons mayonnaise
- ¾ teaspoon celery seed
- ¼ cup cider vinegar
- 1 teaspoon yellow mustard
- 1 tablespoon sugar
- Salt and pepper to taste
- 4oz. radishes, sliced thinly
- 12oz. sugar snap peas, sliced thinly

Directions:

1. In a bowl, combine the mayonnaise, celery seeds, vinegar, mustard, sugar, salt, and pepper.
2. Stir in the radishes and snap peas.
3. Refrigerate for 30 minutes.

Nutrition: Calories: 69; Fat: 4g; Carbohydrates: 7g; Protein: 2g

Preparation Time: 10 Minutes

Cooking Time: 20 Minutes

Servings: 2

Ingredients:

- 1 cup Brown Lentils, dried & cooked
- 30 Cherry Tomatoes, quartered
- 4 Zucchini, rinsed and ends discarded

For the dressing:

- 30 Capers
- 2 Avocado, small & ripe
- 1/2 cup Water
- 1 cup Parsley, fresh
- 1 tsp. Garlic Powder
- Juice of 1 Lemon
- 2 tbsp. Extra Virgin Olive Oil

Directions:

1   For making this healthy salad, you need to make zucchini ribbons by running the vegetable peeler down the entire length of the veggie while pressing it down lightly.

2   Now, combine the zucchini ribbons and quartered cherry tomatoes in a large mixing bowl.

3   Next, blend all the ingredients needed to make the dressing in a high-speed blender for two minutes or until you get a smooth one.

4   Then, check for seasoning and add more as needed.

5   Finally, stir in the cooked lentils and spoon in the dressing over it.

6   Serve and enjoy.

Nutrition: Calories: 462;   Protein: 13g; Carbohydrates: 50g; Fat: 29g

Preparation Time: 5 Minutes

Cooking Time: 0 Minutes

Servings: 2

Ingredients:

For the salad:

- ½ yellow bell pepper, seeded and cut into bite-size pieces
- ½ red onion, peeled and sliced thinly
- ½ cup tofu cheese, cut into bite-size squares
- 10 Kalamata olives pitted
- 3 large tomatoes cut into bite-size pieces
- ½ cucumber, cut into bite-size pieces

For the dressing:

- 4 tbsp olive oil
- ½ tbsp red wine vinegar
- 2 tsp dried oregano
- Salt and black pepper to taste

Directions:

- In a salad bowl, combine all the salad's ingredients until well combined
- In a small bowl, mix the dressing's ingredients and toss into the salad.

- Dish the salad and enjoy!

Nutrition: Calories: 254; Fat: 21g; Carbohydrates: 11;
Protein: 7g

Preparation Time: 10 Minutes

Cooking Time: 25 Minutes

Servings: 4

Ingredients:

- 4 Green Onions, diced
- ½ cup Quinoa, raw
- 2 tbsp. Cilantro
- ½ of 1 Red Bell Pepper, thinly sliced
- ¼ cup Basil, chopped
- 1 Carrot, large & shaved
- ½ cup Cashew, roasted
- 2 cup Kale, packed loosely
- ¾ cup Edamame

For the Thai peanut sauce:

- 2 tbsp. Water
- ¼ cup Natural Peanut Butter
- Pinch of Cayenne
- 2 tbsp. Sesame Oil
- Juice of ½ of 1 Lemon
- 2 tbsp. Soy Sauce
- 1 tsp. Maple Syrup
- 1 tbsp. Rice Vinegar

- 2 Garlic cloves, minced
- 2 tsp. Ginger, fresh & grated

Directions:

1. First, place quinoa and one cup of water in a deep saucepan over medium-high heat and bring the mixture to a boil.
2. Reduce the heat once the mixture starts boiling and allow it to simmer.
3. Simmer the quinoa for 20 to 25 minutes or until all the water has been absorbed.
4. Next, fluff the cooked quinoa with a fork. Set it aside to cool. Once cooled, place the quinoa in the refrigerator.
5. In the meantime, toss all the remaining ingredients together in a large mixing bowl.
6. After that, make the dressing by mixing all the ingredients needed to make the dressing in a large bowl, excluding the water with an immersion blender or blend in a high-speed blender.
7. Blend until you get a smooth, thickened sauce.
8. Add water as needed to get the consistency you desire.
9. Finally, combine the cooled quinoa with the salad and drizzle the peanut sauce over it.

10 Toss well and serve immediately.

Nutrition: Calories: 478; Fat: 36g; Carbohydrates: 29; Protein: 13g

Preparation Time: 10 Minutes

Cooking Time: 25 minutes

Servings: 4

Ingredients:

- 3 cups Lentil
- 3 Parsnips, cut into smaller pieces
- 1 tbsp. Vegetable Stock
- 3 Beetroot, cut into smaller pieces
- 1 tsp. Olive Oil
- 3 Carrots, cut into smaller pieces
- 1 tsp. Balsamic Vinegar
- 2 Red Onion, sliced thinly
- 1 Celeriac, cut into smaller pieces
- ½ tsp. Pepper, grounded
- 4 Garlic cloves, minced
- ½ tsp. Rosemary, dried
- ½ tbsp. Kosher Salt
- 1 tbsp. Black Pepper

Directions:

1   To start with, preheat the oven to 175 °C.

2 After that, transfer the onion, veggies, rosemary, and garlic to a parchment-paper-lined baking sheet.

3 Toss well the veggies with olive oil, ground pepper, and salt.

4 Now, cook them for 35 to 40 minutes or until roasted.

5 In the meantime, cook the lentils in 6 cups of water by following the instructions given on the packet.

6 Once the water starts boiling, spoon in one tablespoon of the vegetable stock.

7 Now, lower the heat and allow the lentils to simmer for 25 minutes.

8 Next, drain the lentils and spoon in the balsamic vinegar and olive oil. Toss well.

9 Top with the roasted veggies and serve immediately.

Nutrition: Calories: 668; Fat: 4g; Carbohydrates: 119g; Protein: 40g

Preparation Time: 25 Minutes

Cooking Time: 10 minutes

Servings: 6

Ingredients:

Salad

- 12 ounces whole-wheat pasta
- 2 cups carrot, peeled and chopped
- 1 cup black olives, pitted and sliced
- 1 cup red bell pepper, seeded and chopped
- 1 cup yellow bell pepper, seeded and chopped
- 1 cup orange bell pepper, seeded and chopped
- ¾ cup fresh cilantro, chopped
- 1 jalapeño pepper, seeded and chopped finely
- 1 cup scallions, chopped

Vinaigrette

- 2 tablespoons balsamic vinegar
- 2 tablespoons extra-virgin olive oil
- 1 tablespoon fresh lemon juice
- 1 teaspoon sesame oil
- 1½ teaspoons red pepper flakes, crushed

Directions:

1. In a pan of salted boiling water, add the pasta and cook for about 8–10 minutes or according to the package's directions.
2. Drain the pasta well and rinse under cold water.
3. Transfer the pasta into a large bowl.
4. Meanwhile, in another pan of salted boiling water, add the edamame and cook for about 5 minutes.
5. Drain the edamame well.
6. In the bowl of pasta, add the edamame and remaining salad ingredients (except scallions) and gently stir to combine.
7. For vinaigrette: in another bowl, add all the ingredients and beat until well combined.
8. Pour the vinaigrette over salad and gently stir to combine.
9. Serve immediately with the garnishing of scallion and sesame seeds.

Nutrition: Calories: 333; Fat: 9g; Protein: 10g; Carbohydrates: 54g

38 Chickpea and Veggie Salad

Preparation Time: 20 Minutes

Cooking Time: 20 minutes

Servings: 2

Ingredients:

- 1 medium avocado, peeled, pitted, and sliced
- 2 teaspoons fresh lime juice
- 2 cups fresh baby spinach
- ¾ cup boiled chickpeas
- 1 cup grape tomatoes
- 1 cup baby carrots
- 1 medium cucumber, sliced
- ¼ cup red onion, sliced
- 2 tablespoons olive oil
- 6 tablespoons hummus
- 2 tablespoons pumpkin seeds

Directions:

1. In a bowl, add the avocado slices and lemon juice and toss to coat well.

2. In the bottom of 2 serving bowls, divide the spinach and top with the chickpeas, vegetables, and avocado slices.

3. Drizzle each bowl with oil and top with hummus.

4. Garnish with pumpkin seeds and serve immediately.

Nutrition: Calories: 611; Fat: 43g; Carbohydrates: 49g; Protein: 14g

Preparation Time: 15 Minutes

Cooking Time: 15 Minutes

Servings: 3

Ingredients:

- 6 teaspoons extra-virgin olive oil
- 2 teaspoons balsamic vinegar
- Salt and ground black pepper, to taste
- 2 cups cooked farro
- 1 cup carrots, peeled and sliced
- 1 cup yellow bell pepper, seeded and chopped
- 1 cup grape tomatoes, halved
- 1 cup cucumber, chopped
- 2 tablespoons fresh cilantro leaves

Directions:

1. In a small bowl, add oil, vinegar, salt, and black pepper, and beat until well combined.
2. In a large bowl, add the remaining ingredients and mix well.
3. Pour the vinaigrette over salad and toss to coat well.
4. Serve immediately.

Nutrition: Calories: 551; Fat: 9g; Carbohydrates: 98g; Protein: 20g

Preparation Time: 20 Minutes

Cooking Time: 5 Minutes

Servings: 4

Ingredients:

Salad

- ½ cup homemade vegetable broth
- ½ cup couscous
- 1 cup frozen corn, thawed
- 3 cups canned red kidney beans, rinsed and drained
- 2 large tomatoes, chopped
- 6 cups fresh spinach, torn

Dressing

- 1 garlic clove, minced
- 2 tablespoons shallots, minced
- 2 teaspoons lemon zest, grated finely
- ¼ cup fresh lemon juice
- 2 tablespoons extra-virgin olive oil
- Salt and ground black pepper, to taste

Directions:

1. In a pan, add the broth over medium heat and bring to a boil.
2. Add the couscous and stir to combine.

3. Cover the pan and immediately remove from the heat.

4. Set aside, covered for about 5–10 minutes, or until all the liquid is absorbed.

5. For salad: in a large serving bowl, add the couscous and remaining ingredients and stir to combine.

6. For dressing: in another small bowl, add all the ingredients and beat until well combined.

7. Pour the dressing over salad and gently toss to coat well.

8. Serve immediately.

Nutrition: Calories: 365; Protein: 19g; Carbohydrates: 58g; Fats: 8g

Preparation Time: 10 Minutes

Cooking Time: 30 Minutes

Servings: 2

Ingredients:

- 2 beets, peeled and thinly sliced
- 1 teaspoon extra-virgin olive oil
- Pinch sea salt
- 1 avocado
- 2 cups mixed greens
- 3 to 4 tablespoons Creamy Balsamic Dressing
- 2 tablespoons chopped almonds, pumpkin seeds, or sunflower seeds (raw or toasted)

Directions:

1 Preparing the Ingredients

2 Preheat the oven to 400°F.

3 Put the beets, oil, and salt in a large bowl, and toss the beets with your hands to coat. Lay them in a single layer in a large baking dish, and roast them in the oven for 20- minutes, or until they're softened and slightly browned around the edges.

4 While the beets are roasting, cut the avocado in half and take the pit out. Scoop the flesh out, as intact as possible, and slice it into crescents.

5 Once the beets are cooked, lay slices out on two plates and top each beet slice with a similar-size avocado slice.

6 Finish and Serve

7 Top with a handful of mixed greens. Drizzle the dressing over everything, and sprinkle on a few chopped almonds.

Nutrition: Calories: 167; Fats: 13g; Carbohydrates: 15g; Protein: 4g

Preparation Time: 5 Minutes

Cooking Time: 15 Minutes

Servings: 4

Ingredients:

- 1 cup brown rice
- ¼ cup olive oil
- ¼ cup orange juice
- 1 pear, cored and diced
- ½ cucumber, diced
- ¼ cup raisins

Directions:

1 Place the rice in a pot with 2 cups of salted water. Bring to a boil, then lower the heat and simmer for 15 minutes.

2 In a bowl, whisk together the olive oil, orange juice, salt, and pepper.

3 Stir in the pear, cucumber, raisins, and cooked rice.

4 Serve.

Nutrition: Calories: 523; Fat: 13g; Carbohydrates: 92g; Protein: 10g

43 Tempeh and Tofu Salad

Preparation Time: 10 Minutes

Cooking Time: 30 Minutes

Servings: 4

Ingredients:

For the tempeh:

- 2 tbsp. Soy Sauce
- 1 tsp. Garlic Powder
- 14 oz. Tempeh
- ¼ cup Balsamic Vinegar
- Salt & Pepper, as needed
- 2 tbsp. Maple Syrup

For the tofu:

- 2 tbsp. Soy Sauce
- 14 oz. Tofu
- 1 tsp. Garlic Powder
- Salt & Pepper, as needed

For the salad:

- 1/3 cup Chickpeas
- 2 tbsp. Hemp Seeds
- 2 tbsp. Tahini
- ¼ of 1 Avocado, large
- ½ of 1 Cucumber, diced

- ¼ of 1 Broccoli, torn

Directions:

- First, we need to season the tempeh by placing all the seasoning required in a large bowl.
- Coat thoroughly and allow the tempeh to get marinated with the flavors either for 2 hours or overnight.
- Next, arrange the seasoned tempeh on a parchment paper-lined baking sheet and bake them for 20 minutes.
- Similarly, marinate the tofu by mixing all the ingredients in a medium bowl.
- Finally, add all the ingredients needed to make the salad in another large mixing bowl.
- To this, stir in the tofu and baked tempeh. Drizzle the lemon juice and tahini paste over it. Coat well.
- Serve and enjoy.

Nutrition: Calories: 619; Protein: 40g; Carbohydrates: 49g; Fat: 33g

Preparation Time: 10 Minutes

Cooking Time: 15 Minutes

Servings: 4

Ingredients:

- A handful of Italian Parsley, fresh
- ½ cup Sunflower Seeds
- 1 cup Dry Quinoa
- 2 tbsp. Olive Oil
- ½ cup Sun-dried Tomatoes, chopped
- ¼ cup Red Onion,
- ¼ cup Dill, fresh
- 4 cups Broccoli Florets
- Juice of 1 Lemon
- 1 ½ cup Chickpeas
- Salt & Pepper, as needed.

Directions:

1   First, place the quinoa in a deep saucepan over medium heat.

2   Next, spoon in red onions, olive oil, and broccoli florets in a medium-sized saucepan.

3   Cook the onion-broccoli for 4 minutes or until the vegetables have softened.

4   Now, place the cooked quinoa along with broccoli, dill, parsley, red onion, sun-dried tomatoes, and chickpeas in a large bowl.

5   Finally, mix everything and drizzle the lemon juice over it.

6   Taste for seasoning. Spoon in more salt and pepper if needed.

7   Serve and enjoy immediately.

Nutrition: Calories: 572; Fat: 17g; Carbohydrates: 84g; Protein: 25g

45 Greek Potato Salad

Preparation Time: 5 Minutes

Cooking Time: 20 Minutes

Servings: 4

Ingredients:

- 6 potatoes, scrubbed or peeled and chopped
- Salt
- ¼ cup extra-virgin olive oil
- 2 tablespoons apple cider vinegar
- 2 tablespoons freshly squeezed lemon juice
- 1 teaspoon dried herbs
- ½ cucumber, chopped
- ¼ red onion, diced
- ¼ cup chopped pitted black olives
- Freshly ground black pepper

Directions:

1 Preparing the Ingredients.

2 Put the potatoes in a large pot, add a pinch of salt, and pour in enough water to cover. Bring the water to boil over high heat. Cook the potatoes for 15-minutes until soft. Drain and set aside to cool. (Alternatively, put the potatoes in a large microwave-safe dish with a bit of water. Cover and heat on high power for 10 minutes.)

3   In a large bowl, whisk together the olive oil, vinegar, lemon juice, and dried herbs. Toss the cucumber, red onion, and olives with the dressing. Add the cooked, cooled potatoes, then toss to combine.

4   Finish and Serve

5   Taste and season with salt and pepper as needed. Store leftovers in an airtight container in the refrigerator for up to 1 week.

Nutrition: Calories: 358; Fat: 16g; Carbohydrates: 52g; Protein: 5g

Preparation Time: 15 Minutes

Cooking Time: 5 minutes

Servings: 3

Ingredients:

- 1 (14-ounce) can black beans, drained and rinsed, or 1½ cups cooked
- 1 cup corn kernels, fresh and blanched, or frozen and thawed
- ¼ cup fresh cilantro, or parsley, chopped
- Zest and juice of 1 lime
- 1 to 2 teaspoons chili powder
- Pinch sea salt
- 1½ cups cherry tomatoes, halved
- 1 red bell pepper, seeded and chopped
- 2 scallions, chopped

For 1 serving of Tortilla Chips

- 1 large whole-grain tortilla or wrap
- 1 teaspoon extra-virgin olive oil
- Pinch sea salt
- Pinch freshly ground black pepper
- Pinch dried oregano
- Pinch chili powder

For 1 bowl:

- 1 cup fresh greens (lettuce, spinach, or whatever you like)
- ¾ cup cooked quinoa, or brown rice, millet, or other whole grain
- ¼ cup chopped avocado, or guacamole
- ¼ cup Fresh Mango Salsa

Directions:

1 To make the black bean salad
2 Toss all the ingredients together in a large bowl.
3 To make the tortilla chips
4 Brush the tortilla with olive oil, then sprinkle with salt, pepper, oregano, chili powder, and any other seasonings you like. Slice it into eighths like a pizza.
5 Transfer the tortilla pieces to a small baking sheet lined with parchment paper and put in the oven or toaster oven to toast, or broil for 3-5 minutes until browned. Keep an eye on them as they can go from just barely done to burned very quickly.
6 To make the bowl
7 Lay the greens in the bowl, top with the cooked quinoa, ⅓ of the black bean salad, the avocado, and salsa.

Nutrition: Calories: 589; Fat: 14g; Carbohydrates: 101g; Protein: 21g

Preparation Time: 10 Minutes

Cooking Time: 50 minutes

Servings: 4

Ingredients:

- 1 teaspoon extra-virgin olive oil plus ¼ cup, divided, or 1 tablespoon vegetable broth or water
- 1 small onion, diced
- 1 garlic clove, minced
- 1 carrot, diced
- 1 cup lentils
- 1 tablespoon dried basil
- 1 tablespoon dried oregano
- 1 tablespoon red wine or balsamic vinegar (optional)
- 2 cups water
- ¼ cup red wine vinegar or balsamic vinegar
- 1 teaspoon sea salt
- 2 cups chopped Swiss chard
- 2 cups torn red leaf lettuce
- 4 tablespoons Cheesy Sprinkle

Directions:

1   Heat 1 teaspoon of the oil in a large pot on medium heat, then sauté the onion and garlic until they are translucent.

2   Add the carrot and sauté until it is slightly cooked. Stir in the lentils, basil, and oregano, then add the wine or balsamic vinegar (if using).

3   Pour the water into the pot and turn the heat up to high to bring to boil.

4   Turn the heat down to a simmer and let the lentils cook, uncovered, for 20-30 minutes until they are soft but not falling apart.

5   While the lentils are cooking, whisk together the red wine vinegar, olive oil, and salt in a small bowl and set aside. Once the lentils have cooked, drain any excess liquid and stir in most of the red wine vinegar dressing. Set a little bit of dressing aside. Add the Swiss chard to the pot and stir it into the lentils. Leave the heat on low and cook, stirring, for at least 10 minutes.

6   Toss the lettuce with the remaining dressing. Place some lettuce on a plate, and top with the lentil mixture. Finish the plate off with a little cheesy sprinkle and enjoy.

Nutrition: Calories: 387; Fat: 17g; Protein: 18g; Carbohydrates: 42g

Preparation Time: 10 Minutes

Cooking Time: 50 minutes

Servings: 4

Ingredients:

- 1 large tomato, diced
- 1 red bell pepper, diced
- 1 green bell pepper, diced
- 1 small red onion, diced
- 1 (14.5-ounce) can black-eyed peas, rinsed and drained
- 1 (14.5-ounce) can black beans, rinsed and drained
- 1 (14.5-ounce) can yellow corn, rinsed and drained
- 2 avocados, pitted
- 2 tablespoons lemon juice (about 1 small lemon)
- ¼ cup unseasoned rice vinegar, apple cider vinegar, or white wine vinegar
- 1 teaspoon dried oregano
- ½ teaspoon salt
- 8 cups loosely packed leafy greens (kale, spinach, arugula, or romaine lettuce), divided

Directions:

1. In a large bowl, combine the tomato, peppers, onion, black-eyed peas, beans, and corn. Set aside.

2. In a blender, purée the avocados, lemon juice, vinegar, oregano, and salt to make a creamy dressing.

3. Into each of 4 wide-mouth quart jars, spoon about 2 tablespoons of the dressing. Add about 1¼ cups "caviar" followed by 2 cups of leafy greens to each. Seal the lids tightly.

Nutrition: Calories: 411; Fat: 16g; Carbohydrates: 60g; Protein: 16g

49 Creamed Green Bean Salad with Pine Nuts

Preparation Time: 10 Minutes

Cooking Time: 2 Minutes

Servings: 5

Ingredients:

- 1 ½ pounds green beans, trimmed
- 2 medium tomatoes, diced
- 2 bell peppers, seeded and diced
- 4 tablespoons shallots, chopped
- 1/2 cup pine nuts, roughly chopped
- 1/2 cup vegan mayonnaise
- 1 tablespoon deli mustard
- 2 tablespoons fresh basil, chopped
- 2 tablespoons fresh parsley, chopped
- 1/2 teaspoon red pepper flakes, crushed
- Sea salt and freshly ground black pepper, to taste

Directions:

1 Boil the green beans in a large saucepan of salted water until they are just tender or about 2 minutes.

2 Drain and let the beans cool completely; then, transfer them to a salad bowl. Toss the beans with the remaining ingredients.

3   Taste and adjust the seasonings. Bon appétit!

Nutrition: Calories: 308; Fat: 26g; Carbohydrates: 16g; Protein: 6g

Preparation Time: 5 Minutes

Cooking Time: 10 Minutes

Servings: 4

Ingredients:

- 1 ½ pounds green beans, trimmed
- 1/2 cup scallions, chopped
- 1 teaspoon garlic, minced
- 1 Persian cucumber, sliced
- 2 cups grape tomatoes, halved
- 1/4 cup olive oil
- 1 teaspoon deli mustard
- 2 tablespoons tamari sauce
- 2 tablespoons lemon juice
- 1 tablespoon apple cider vinegar
- 1/4 teaspoon cumin powder
- 1/2 teaspoon dried thyme
- Sea salt and ground black pepper, to taste

Directions:

1   Boil the green beans in a large saucepan of salted water until they are just tender or about 2 minutes.

2   Drain and let the beans cool completely; then, transfer them to a salad bowl. Toss the beans with the remaining ingredients.

3   Bon appétit!

Nutrition: Calories: 240; Protein: 4g; Carbohydrates: 29g; Fats: 14g

CPSIA information can be obtained
at www.ICGtesting.com
Printed in the USA
BVHW061017220321
603175BV00003B/145